Forever Growing

Chloe Privett

Presentation by *BookLeaf Publishing*

Web: www.bookleafpub.com

E-mail: info@bookleafpub.com

ISBN: 9789395756488

First edition 2022

DEDICATION

This book is dedicated to my 2 gorgeous Boys. My world revolves around them and it forever will, I'm so grateful to call them mine. Also my niece, this is to show them all that anything is possible.

Thank you Finley, Oliver and Ella for showing me what love and life truly means. I love you all the moon and all the stars in the world xxxxxxx

ACKNOWLEDGEMENT

Firstly, I would like to thank my mum, my sister Emma and my family, for this opportunity and supporting me of my writing all these years and my life achievements, you are, our village. Without your guidance and advice over the years, we would be lost without you all and I would not be the person I am today. xxx

Secondly, I want to thank my husband Aaron, for looking after the boys in the evenings and weekends, to allow me the time and dedication to write this book. And just being amazing in every way! You have always supported me, you are the best daddy to our boys. Us three are very lucky, we love you xxxxxxx

Lastly, to all the family members we have lost along the years, who will always hold a very special place in my heart. They have all had such key roles to me in my lifetime, and impacted me significantly. Rest in Paradise xxx

PREFACE

I have been through some emotional journeys to say the least. I have lost a few family members close to my heart, lost a few friends a long the way. Found who I want to grow old and build a life with. And furthermore, recently entered the world of motherhood, with having a 22month age gap between both my children, I'm currently on Maternity leave as I write this book. I hope that this book can relate to others and what they may have experienced in life as well.

Lost Without You...

I thought you would be here forever,
Did I imagine life without you, never,
From diagnosis, to you being gone,
It really was not very long,
It was tough and hard to see,
Even your last days, you still smiled with me,
You showed me strength,
You showed me courage, to be brave,
I watched you fight until the very end,
I was lucky to have you in my life,
You made everyone you knew, days so bright
There is an empty space in my heart,
Because the day you left, we all fell apart,
Life without you around, is not the same,
I'm learning to deal with it every single day,
They say that time is a healer,
But in reality it doesn't get any easier.

Stay With Me...

We stand beside your bedside and watch you
peacefully sleep,
Those happy dreams you are dreaming,
Whilst we stand aside and weep,
You open your eyes and look around,
Our voices being a familiar sound,
Giving you a cuddle and a kiss,
Which soon we are sadly going to miss,
We love you so very dear,
Loosing you is our fear,
You are so strong and very brave,
We are by your side everyday,
Every minute, Every hour are such precious
time,
Why is it you, that is next in line,
I'd travel the sea,
I'd fly across the sky,
I'd do anything, for you to stay nearby,
I'd trek up mountains,
I'd walk for endless miles,
Just to keep seeing that infectious smile,
I know it is time soon, to turn off the light,
You have taut me to never give up, without a
fight.

Wish You Were Here...

As each year passes it gets harder and harder,
There are milestones you have missed, which
you would have been apart of,
It's been so long since hearing your voice,
Your words of wisdom or helpful advice,
I just wish I could have you back in our life,

The memories I have, I will treasure forever,
As I was grateful to have known you in our
lifetime together,
The long phone calls that we used to have,
Knowing I can't ring you, just makes me so sad,
I don't think you realised how many lives you
made brighter,
With your infectious smile and caring nature,

The more occasions you miss, I wish you were
here,
Guiding me through, or telling me how to stay
clear,
It gives me hope, in thinking you are near,
I see Robins on my walks, or I have white
feathers appear,
Everything I do, I try and make you proud,
I hope you are watching from above on your
cloud.

Not Just Bricks...

The sun is shining through the car,
I feel the warmth on my skin,
I'm aimlessly driving around,
Next thing I'm on a familiar road,
Yet it all looks different,
All the plants & bushes have overgrown,
There's your house, but I can't go in,
Oh what I would do to knock that door,
For you to answer just once more,
I feel close to you when I am here,
The bricks are all I have to feel you near,
Inside those walls my childhood was created,
50years of a family generation in the making,
We didn't just lose you, we lost much more,
But it is time for another family to walk through the door,
Your house is one I will cherish forever,
I will always drive by if I am in the area.

Our Twenties...

As time goes on, it gets a little harder,
Seeing photos of your memories, I wish I was
apart of,
We used to be each others right wing,
Dancing on tables, me getting the shots in,
Ladies toilet selfies, hitting on the bouncers,
Pre drinks at your place, Getting out the taxi and
fallen flat on my face,
Cinema dates, trips to the beach,
Eating our body weight in ice cream,
I'm not quite sure where it went pear shaped,
We just grew at different rates,
I owe you for all the flashbacks we have,
From helping through heartbreak, to finding the
best I've ever had,
My late teens with you were so memorable,
However without this friendship, I cannot help
feel sorrow,
I wish you nothing more than the very best,
But maybe one day, we're catch up where we
left...

Strangers For Now...

We stop and speak to each other on the street,
A generic chat about how we have been,
Off we go in our separate ways,
Wondering when did it all change,
We used to be the best of friends,
We would tell each other everything,
There through school, college and careers,
I am not really sure how it got to this,
We took different routes and lost our way,
Hopeful we may join back up one day,
For now you are a stranger, that goes by,
Seeing your life, by what you post online,
I see you still go to festivals and gigs,
That used to be our thing, that's what we did,
I hope your happy in whatever you do,
I hope will we get to rekindle someday soon.

Butterflies...

My phone pings with a notification,
Oh I've matched with another person,
My stomachs in flutters to check them out,
Is this who I've waited for my whole life,
Ping, my phone goes again,
You have one message from your new matched
friend,
Is this just going to be wasted time,
Will it be more of those cheesy chat up lines,
We start to message back and forth,
It seems we actually have a vibe,
The more we chat, I find out more,
Our Interests and dislikes are identical,
And a big bonus is that they live local,
It seems we like the same foods, music and
holidays,
And there is even talks about our future one day,
When my phone pings, I get excited,
Butterflies in my tummy, there's no feeling like
it,
Every time we talk, I learn something new,
I already feel a connection, I hope they do to,
I'm enjoying talking and getting to know them,
Perhaps very soon we will arrange a date…

When You Know...

When I saw you,
My gut said you are the one,
When I got to know you,
I completely fell in love,
All these years of having you by my side,
All these years of being proud your all mine,
There is a lot we have been through,
And a lot we have overcome,
But through it all, you remain my number one,

Il never forget meeting all your family,
I was so scared and nervous, yet now I fit in,
Moving in together and finding our habits,
That was a daily occurrence that certainly tested
us,
We have similar interests give or take,
Each concert we attend, another memory we
make,
From planning our wedding, to the day itself,
A dream had turned into reality it felt,

Marriage has certainly brought us closer,
There is no way I could navigate life without
you,

We have both lost family along the way,
Supported, grieved with one another on our sad
days,
You truly have become my best friend,
What we have is such a special bond.

Is This The One...

Driving around looking for boards,
Dreaming one day it will be yours,
Searching the area, to see if I get any feels,
I hope soon my dreams, will turn very real,
Countless scrolling on different sites,
Comparing which ones are reasonably priced,
Some too much work, some too small,
I'm suddenly realising what I want after all,
A nice sized garden, to be out in the sun,
Maybe a utility room, to get washing done,
A loft conversion, would be a bonus,
But a decent drive would be what would sway
us,
I'm not really sure if we have enough in the
budget,
I just hope there's enough the bank would lend
us,
Viewings are booked, it all feels very surreal,
Could this be our forever home, when we walk
through that door.

Forever Growing...

Laughter heard from another room,
Toys scattered along the playroom floor,
Losing site of adulthood even more,
Pictures hung with crayons been drawn,
It looks like a play park all over our lawn,
When cupboards open, little snacks fall out,
One is full of Tupperware, without the lids no doubt,
Our wine rack currently used as a toy car garage,
There will be a time we look back and we will miss it,
Washing ready, to load in the machine,
Bottles in soak, ready for sterilising,
House plants scattered, barely green,
On the kitchen side is a cold cup of tea,
Toys found in the most unusual places,
A toddler and baby, putting us through our paces,
This is not just a house, but our family home,
Where dancing in the kitchen, is all we have ever known,
This is our safe place, our humble abode,
Where each year in here, the love has just grown,
I would not change this house for the world,
So many memories here, and so many more to occur.

Miracles Do Happen...

Il never forget seeing you on that screen,
Wriggling around inside of me,
Who are you & what will you be,
I can't believe this miracle is happening,
I have dreamt of this moment over and over,
Now my dreams are reality its just so joyous,
As each week passes on by,
I bond with you, I cannot deny,
The love I have for you is second to none,
We may not have met yet, but you are my
number one,
My tummy is getting bigger and my face is
getting fuller,
My body is creating a home for you to feel safe
in,
Some aches and pains, also stretch marks
appearing,
It's not bothering me, I just pray that you are
healthy,
There are so many emotions you ride along the
way,
Will I be a good mum? Will everything be ok,
The sickness, the moods and leaky boobs to,
There is no doubt in my mind, I would do it all
again for you,

I get to carry you for 9 whole months,
It may feel like a lifetime, but it is not that long,
As the due date is nearing, everything is in
place,
All ready and set, to see your gorgeous face.

You Got This...

Will I be a good mum,
When will I know to change their bum,
How will I know when to feed them,
Do I set an alarm clock, or will they let me
know,
They've started to cry, what does it mean,
How do I know if they even like me,
What shall I do at home, if I need a wee,
As for nappies, what size should they be,
Bottles, teats, nipples and shields,
I'm clueless and ready to run for the hills,
Comparing their Poo colour online to see,
You don't even want to see my Google History,
Is it normal for babies to do this amount of wee,
Oh gosh they have a rash, what could this be,
What age do babies even start to wean,
People keep asking me what's our routine?
No question is too silly, so ask them please,
One thing I've learned is there's no wrong or
right way,
It can be totally different from yesterday to
today,
The fact that you worry and are open for advice,
Just proves that anyone would be lucky, to have
you as their mum.

Clockwork...

15

I look at the clock, it is 3am,
Why is this baby not sleeping again,
Daylight emerges and birds begin to sing,
The morning has arrived, and I'm already done in,
I watch the clock hour by hour,
When my partner gets home, they can take over,
"Here have the baby, I am off for a shower",
The water drops down and it is peace and quiet,
I should now feel relaxed but I just feel guilty,
I must get back to the baby, after 2minutes of tranquillity,
Bedtime routine has all gone smoothly,
Bath, milk and put down to bed,
I look at the clock, it's 3am,
I start this whole circle all over again.

Time Waster...

I can stare at your face for hours and hours,
Time wasters is what they say,
But I am just so proud of who you are today,
I grew you inside my tummy,
And I now have the privilege of being your
mummy,
When we cuddle, you hold me tight,
Through the day or throughout the night,
I have never experienced love like this,
There is nothing I ever want to miss,
You are half of your dad, half of me,
We have created the perfect recipe,
From your cute ears, to your tiny toes,
Each hair on your body,
You take away all my woes,
Being in my arms, in a familiar place,
Wishing you could stay here, forever safe,
Sometimes I watch when you are asleep,
Wondering about how the future will be,
Because it will be down to you to hold your key,
And all I want is for you to be happy.

Best Role Model...

You are by my side, through the whole 9
months,
Not feeling anything, but movement in my tum,
To watch me go through all the emotions,
To fulfilling my weird craving creations,
Suddenly from nowhere, a baby in your arms,
You feel like protecting, like a queen's guard,
That first ride home, you drove so slow,
Avoiding all the bumps along the roads,
Those first few weeks trying to find our feet,
Whilst entering the new world of parenting,
You were so amazing at looking after me,
Watching you become a dad, was just the best to
see,

We wait for you daily to come home from work,
Seeing them in your car window, i see your
smirk,
It must feel strange to leave the house all day,
To come home to little ones wanting to play,
For the roof is on our head, because of you,
Working hard for our family, getting us through,
You cook, you clean, bath and bed routine,
You help every day and never leave it down to
me,

You have just flourished in your role as Daddy,
It's so natural, like you were always meant to be,

I am the proudest I have ever been,
We have such a beautiful life and family,
I can't thank you enough for looking after the
boys and me,
The best role model for them, you will be.

Slow Down Time...

People told me, time flies when you have
children,
And when I was pregnant, I just never believed
them,
But now that you are already a toddler,
I've blinked and 2years has passed us,
There is a lot we have been through together,
You have made me change as a person, for the
better,
I love my time spent with you,
I wish I could keep you little forever,
You're growing bigger as each day goes by,
But I never knew, the wrong cup could make
someone cry,
Terrible two's are quite interesting, I'm not
going to lie,
You have become my little best mate,
We do everything together, from morning to
night,
I love seeing you explore something new,
My heart could burst, the love I have for you,
You are such a happy little soul,
Everyday I hear new words unfold,
Im truly lucky that you are mine,
But right now I wish, I could slow down time.

Complete...

How will I cope with two of you,
Will your sibling love you, as much as I do,
Will my heart get bigger with pride,
Or will I lose myself against the tide,

I'm excited, scared, happy and nervous,
There will not be much gap, but I have got this,
For you are my second but also my last,
I will cherish these moments and never be sad,

Things will be different with two around,
My time will be split between you both now,
My heart could just burst for the love I have,
To be your mum, makes me so proud,

Before your arrival, I felt worry and fear,
But the moment I held you, it all disappeared,
For you have completed us, a family of four,
My wish came true, you gave me so much more.

My Tribe...

Signing up to an app, for new mums to be,
It may be wasted time, but lets find out to see,
A few of us on the group start to chat,
All about life, jobs, this and that,
We all get on well and have the same vibe,
So we all swap numbers and create our Tribe,

They say it takes a village and this is mine,
They're a special bunch of mums, who I've met
online,
We are all from different parts of the UK,
And I hope we'll all meet up one day,

Everyday we all talk,
From how to wean or babies learning to walk,
We support and encourage,
No judgement here,
It's a place to vent or to shed a tear,
What we have created, is something special,
Become friends for life, sharing great advice,
Birthdays, achievements they never get missed,
This tribe is more than I ever wished.

Organised Chaos...

The more clothes I wash,
The pile just gets bigger,
Plates start to stack up,
I've just unloaded the dishwasher,
Crumbs all on the floor,
I've just put away the Hoover,
Bills through the door,
I've just sent last months over,
Food shop ordered,
I've got a few treats, like i'm being rewarded,
MOT is running out,
I've just brought the appointment forward,
Birthdays this month,
I've posted the cards,
RSVP's been replied to,
I've sent my regards,
So much on my mind, cannot get to sleep,
I've got a family to look after and a house to
keep,
Kettle is boiled and a cuppa has been made,
I've got to drink it hot quickly, before its to late,
Lots to get on with and lots to do,
I've got to carry on going, I am the glue,
Everything gets prepped the night before,
I've got a tight ship or we'll end up ashore,
Organised chaos, this is family life,
Drowning in jobs, just trying to get them right.

Stop Criticising...

So why are mother's so harshly criticised,
It is one night out, i'm not cutting ties,
Why can't all parents just sympathise,
And we all show the good parts, but never the
bad,
This job is by far the hardest I've had,

I should not admit that it can get a bit tough,
For it just leaves me vulnerable enough,
Social media can print a pretty image,
Of how we should dress or how our child should
be,
Remember they only show, what they want us to
see,

The love for my children is unexplainable,
My heart could burst of how proud I am of them,
But there are times I have felt lonely, yet I am
never alone,
No adult conversations, no friends to phone,
Theres no way I could just ring them to moan?

Mums supporting mums, is what motherhood
should be about,
Not criticising each other, if one goes out,

That could be her sanity to her mental health,
Just delete all those unrealistic parenting
accounts,
You need a team, people behind your back,
So lets start being real, maybe then no one will
judge.

Forever Job...

For this is my new role,
My very first day,
No experience needed,
No reference they say,
Where is the manual to read beforehand,
Surely there is an induction to get my head
around,

Just like that, no 9 till 5,
It is 24 / 7, but you will survive,
Breaks are forbidden,
Holidays are frowned,
You want time to yourself,
That's certainly not allowed,

This role sounds hard, one you won't control,
Every day a new mother gets to enrol,
But nobody feels like they need to explain,
Each person just ends up finding their way,

There is more responsibilities, than you ever
knew before,
Just keep your head above water or try to stay
ashore,
There is no guide, for if you are doing it right,

You do what works best, to get you through day
and night,

This job is hard, that may be an understatement,
However there are so many Pro's to having
children,
You gain this love you never knew existed,
They show you a new life that you have always
wished for,

For this role does not include trophies and
medals,
It shows you what you are truly made of,
To have a beautiful family, I feel so blessed,
This job is forever, by no means a test.